LANDSCAPE SEQUEN
1983-6

C000119167

Cover Illustration: Labyrinth 4

Triptych 2

LANDSCAPE SEQUENCES
1983-6

ELIZABETH WILLIAMS

ASHMOLEAN MUSEUM, OXFORD
1986

Exhibition Venues

The Ashmolean Museum, Oxford   2nd November 1986 – 4th January 1987

Camden Arts Centre, London   9th April – 12th May 1987

Galerie Photographique Vrais Rêves, Lyon, France   November 1987

The exhibition will also tour photographic centres in France

Set in Helvetica Light and printed in England by Cheney & Sons Limited, Banbury, Oxfordshire.

Acknowledgements

Elizabeth Williams would like to thank The Ashmolean Museum, especially The Keeper of Western Art, Dr. Nicholas Penny and the Publications Officer, Ian Charlton; Camden Arts Centre, especially Jeanette Jackson; the Galerie Photographique Vrais Rêves, especially Raymond Viallon; The British Council, especially Brett Rogers (London) and Catherine Ferbos (Paris); Southern Arts Association; Ken Davidson, Ilford Customer Technical Service; Peter Agius; the translator; and her friends, family and colleagues who have helped and encouraged her to make these photographs.

. . . I thought I was going to be a painter.

When did you become interested in photography?

Not until I left Birmingham College of Art. I started writing rather bad poetry, and then I saw some photographs by Robert Frank and Paddy Summerfield, which led me to understand how photographs could function at the same level as paintings.

You had been making large abstract paintings – you mentioned Rothko and Newman as influences. This type of painting was presented as the purest form of art, but it must have entailed a tremendous commitment.

Yes. My particular problem was that I found it hard to work from my own ideas in isolation. I found myself more stimulated by what I saw on my bus journey to the studio, than by the marks that I had made on my canvas! I needed to respond to something outside of myself, and photography provided me with the ideal medium to do this.

The work in this exhibition, and illustrated in this catalogue, dates from the last three years. Before that your photographs – I am thinking especially of the sequences of studies of light on stone walls – were severe and flatter.

Yes, those photographs were uncompromisingly abstract. My work is more figurative now, It's all opened out a lot. My subject matter has a wider variety, and so does the emotional range. I also use a more varied photographic language, in tonality, depth of field. . . .

What about scale? I notice your sequences are sometimes as large as abstract expressionist paintings, which is ideal for the exhibition gallery, but it's unlikely people are going to buy them for their own homes.

Well, recently I have been making prints, to order, at smaller sizes, but I think that they are strongest at 11-16½ inches. I want people to be able to relate to their physical presence. I print them as large as I can from a 35mm negative, without the grain of the negative showing like a screen and obscuring the reality of the grass or tree. . . .

The reality is important for you, as you say, but it is mundane, in a sense – nature as available to all of us.

I've always photographed everyday things, even before I began photographing landscape. I'd rather try to see commonplace things in a new way than photograph strange and exotic things.

The way you present nature deprives it of conventional space. Among the recent sequences only Labyrinth *has anything of the conventional depth of painted landscapes – and even there it is a bewildering space.*

This was quite deliberate. I want to make flat surfaces, but refer to reality by adding a slight illusion of space. The lack of perspective stems not only from my interest in abstract expressionism, but also from icons and chinese painting.

I wondered about Monet?

Yes, Monet is a recent influence.

Monet was also interested in sequences. Like his series, your series of images are suggested by changes in nature. The network of branches which you photograph against the sky develops or loses leaves as the seasons change, or it may be that the weather changes the look of the same piece of water – but, are some of the changes in the sequences due to the way you develop or print, rather than changes in nature itself?

Well, each image is from a different negative. . . .

But you told me that sometimes you make a different image by reversing a negative and using different print manipulation.

Oh, I forgot that! Yes, I did do that in the *Illuminated* sequence.

It's a rather revealing mistake.

Yes. I'm so used to thinking of each photograph as an entirely new image.

When you decide what is right in a print, are you trying to be true to your experience of nature?

I don't aim to produce documentary photographs. I feel quite justified in distorting tones for example, but when I get problems in editing I do try to remember my original experience. . . .

You go back to the local pond or wherever?

Yes, I have done, sometimes.

You feel at ease distorting tones, but you never crop the negative.

This isn't because I'm against cropping on principle. I like the edge that my negative carrier gives the print. It's very soft and makes the image seem to bleed into the paper – and I'm very used to thinking in rectangles now. If I started cropping it would open up so many possibilities that I'd never complete anything.

What about the poetic, even symbolic dimension suggested by your titles – you call one sequence Labyrinth, not, for example, Tangles.

The poetic and spiritual content is very important to me. If the photographs don't work at this level, then I won't use them. I'd like the photographs to function like poetry or music, to calm minds and stimulate thoughts and feelings – something to lose yourself in. . . .

Sequences

*Illuminated	1-8	1983-6
Staying Centred	1-4	1983-4
In Veiled Stillness	1-3	1983-4
*Through a Cycle of Time	1-4	1983-5
Weathering the Storm	1-5	1983-5
Beyond the Boundary Line	1-3	1984-5
*Moving Inwards	1-3	1984-5
Triptych	1-3	1983-6
*Labyrinth	1-4	1983-6

*Illustrated in catalogue.

Illuminated 1

Illuminated 2

Illuminated 3

Illuminated 4

Illuminated 5

Illuminated 6

Illuminated 7

Illuminated 8

Through a Cycle of Time 1

Through a Cycle of Time 2

Through a Cycle of Time 3

Through a Cycle of Time 4

Labyrinth 1

Labyrinth 2

Labyrinth 3

Labyrinth 4

Moving Inwards 1

Moving Inwards 2

27

Moving Inwards 3

Biography

1949   Born in England.

1956-68   Lived in Hampshire. Influenced by Van Gogh and Turner's paintings.

1967-68   Studied at Winchester School of Art.
Influenced by Chinese landscape painting.

1968-71   Studied painting at Birmingham College of Art.
Influenced by Rothko and Newman's abstract expressionist paintings.

1971-72   Wrote poetry. Saw photographs by Robert Frank and Paddy Summerfield.

1972-75   Studied creative photography at London College of Printing.
Influenced by the photographs of Atget, Cameron, Weston and Callahan.

1974   First exhibition, 'New Photography', Midland Group Gallery, Nottingham.

1975   Moved to Oxford. Studied art education at Reading University.

1976   Influenced by Rembrandt's sequence of self-portraits.

1977   Started teaching photography. Saw photographic sequences by Duane Michals.

1978   Began to make sequences.
First individual exhibition, The Photographic Gallery, Southampton.

1980   Influenced by icon painting and the photographs of Sudek, Siskind,
and Thomas Cooper.

1982   First publication of a portfolio, by 'European Photography'.
Exhibited sequences with John Blakemore's landscape sequences.

1983   Began to make landscape sequences.

1985   First purchase of a sequence, by Angela Flowers Gallery, London.

1985   Influenced by Monet's painting at Giverny. Began to photograph in colour.

Group Exhibitions include:

1977	'Summer Show 4', Serpentine Gallery, London. (Arts Council)
1977/78	Hexagon Gallery, Reading.
1979	Rencontres Internationales de la Photographie, Arles, France.
1979/82	International Exhibition of Photography, Zadar, Yugoslavia.
1982	Stadelijk Museum de Lakenhal, Leiden, Holland.
1984	'Form and Feeling', Angela Flowers Gallery, London.
1984	'Contemporary British Abstract Photography', Rochdale Art Gallery.
1984	'Pacesetters 4', Peterborough City Museum and Art Gallery.
1984-5	'Sequences', Cambridge Darkroom & Watershed, Bristol.
1985	'Aspects of Photography', Eastthorpe Gallery, Yorkshire.
1985	'4 Women, 4 Walls', Somerville College, Oxford.
1986	'Surveying the Scene', South Hill Park & Aspex Gallery, Portsmouth.
1986	'16 Studios', Museum of Modern Art, Oxford.
1986	Anniversary Exhibition, Camden Arts Centre, London.
1986	'Man and the Sea', Art Gallery, Peoples Museum, Zadar, Yugoslavia.
1987	The Print Room, The Photographers Gallery, London, & touring.

Individual Exhibitions include:

1978	The Photographic Gallery, Southampton.
1979	'79 International Photographic Conference, Camden Arts Centre, London.
1982	Impressions Gallery of Photography, York.
1983	Photographers Above the Rainbow, Bristol.
1984	Christ Church Picture Gallery, Oxford.
1984-5	The Photographic Centre, Athens, & touring Greece & Cyprus. (British Council).
1985	Bampton Arts Centre, Oxford.
1986	The Print Room, The Photographers Gallery, London.
1986	Minister of Arts Office, House of Parliament, London.
1986	The Ashmolean Museum, Oxford.
1987	Camden Arts Centre, London.
1987-8	Galerie Photographique Vrais Rêves, Lyon, France, and touring.

Awards include:

1977	Southern Arts Association Bursary Award
1979	Southern Arts Association Grant
1979/82	Prizewinner, International Exhibition of Photography, Zadar.
1981	Commission, Light and Line, Printdealers.
1985	Southern Arts Association Grant.